Personal Development

MW01530812

TABLE OF CONTENTS

Cover Art by
Matthew Archambault

Black & White Illustrations by
Ken Landgraf

EDCON
Publishing Group

Copyright © 2006
AV Concepts Corporation
Edcon Publishing Group

Printed in U.S.A.
ISBN# 1-55576-387-1

EDCON PUBLISHING

COURSE
SELECTION

COURSE SELECTION

"I just remembered...in two weeks we have to select our courses for next year. What's everybody taking?" Manny asked his friends over lunch.

"I'm taking the same courses that Frank and Lou take–whatever they are," said Eddie.

Frank and Lou laughed. Manny said jokingly, "Sounds like you're really making up your own mind!" He turned to Betty. "Betty, what courses are you taking?"

"Well, I've made up *my* mind," answered Betty. "I'm taking the easiest courses possible. All I want to do is pass on out of this joint."

"Yeah, I guess it's nothing to get excited about," responded Manny.

COURSE SELECTION

Today's schools offer a wide range of opportunities which students can use to help them prepare for their future. Selecting courses is serious business. It can mean the difference between a happy, productive life, or one that is sad and unrewarding.

Students can select from several curriculum areas:

1. **Academic or Business Prep**
2. **Business**
3. **Vocational**

Each curriculum area has a fixed number of courses that must be taken in order to graduate from high school. For example, if your school requires 22 credits to graduate, you might need to take these courses for the specified amount of time.

Subject	Years
English	4
Social Studies	3
Humanities & Art	2
Mathematics	3
Science	3
Physical Education	1.5
Health	.5

And you would be able to take 5 electives.

EDCON PUBLISHING

COURSE SELECTION

"Ruby, why did you select the College Prep program?" asked Mike. "I thought you wanted to take a business course."

"Well, I just couldn't make up my mind," answered Ruby, "so, I talked to Mr. Shank, the guidance counselor. He suggested that I take the College Prep program because it's easier to switch from College Prep to Business if I change my mind later.

"Then he signed me up for his Career Decision-Making/ Career Exploration Workshop. He said I needed more information about myself and the world of work. He said his Workshop would provide me with SELF INFORMATION and CAREER INFORMATION.

"I want to take the most useful courses I can while I'm still in high school. My sister is going to a Community College, and she has to pay for all her courses. She could have taken those same courses here, last year, for nothing!

"So, Mike, why don't you talk to Mr. Shank?"

COURSE SELECTION

"Yeah. Maybe I'll do that during my study hall. See you later, Ruby."

By visiting her counselor, Ruby was able to develop a drop-back option that would permit her to switch from an academic to a business curriculum at a later date.

If undecided, always take the curriculum that requires the largest number of courses.

Use your counselors as resource people. They will review your grades and test scores and look for patterns of achievements on which you can build your future. They won't make decisions for you. That's YOUR job. But, they can alert you to future employment trends, post-secondary educational requirements, refer you to sources for career information, and explain the decision-making process to you.

You must learn to use the following 6 steps for collecting data and making your decision. Copy them down for later use.

> 1. **COLLECT INFORMATION**
> 2. **ANALYZE INFORMATION**
> 3. **PREPARE ALTERNATIVES**
> 4. **CONSIDER OUTCOMES**
> 5. **SELECT ALTERNATIVES**
> 6. **EVALUATE RESULTS**

Your first task will be to collect PERSONAL data or SELF INFORMATION. Your activities will provide insight into your interests. For example, do you like individual events like track or swimming, or team sports like basketball and football? Do you have artistic ability or creative talents? Do you like to work on cars? Is reading a hobby? What are your favorite school subjects?

EDCON PUBLISHING

Collecting information about the thousands of jobs in the world of work requires you to do some research.

Your career center, school, or local library will have current resource information. It's the place to begin your search. Review the Occupational Outlook Handbook to get an idea of the types of career fields, as well as information available on each occupation.

Read individual pamphlets and flyers on occupations, paying particular attention to the specific educational requirements for each occupation. This will help you when you are ready to select your curriculum area and individual courses.

Occupations have been divided into 15 clusters. Review these clusters and select two or three for further exploration. This will help make the selection process easier.

Within each occupational cluster, a particular occupation can generally be classified in 3 ways – occupations that require working with

1. data.
2. people.
3. things.

Think about these areas and decide whether you fit into one more than another. Are you efficient with numbers, math, and data? If you like meeting and working with people, then you might consider a career in the human services area.

Many occupations require you to have an aptitude and interest in *several* areas. Be sure to look for these combinations when you collect your career material.

Other things to consider about an occupation are the PHYSICAL REQUIREMENTS of the job.

Must you do heavy lifting? If so, how heavy and how much?

COURSE SELECTION

Is climbing involved?
How much and how high?

Do you need special skills –
like knowing how to ride a
horse?

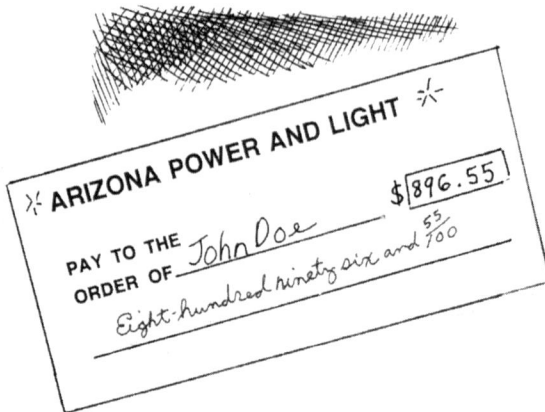

Also, how much will you
earn when you start, and
after several years on the
job? And what are the
benefits? Will you be
paid for holidays? Will
you be paid for sick
leave? What about
health insurance?

EDCON PUBLISHING

Is the work environmently safe?

Will you work inside?

Or outside?

COURSE SELECTION

What are the actual duties required to perform the job? Must you drive heavy equipment? Leap tall buildings? Or run errands for the boss?

Review the job descriptions carefully. Use several sources and personal interviews if necessary.

Consider the employment opportunities. Is it a growing career field? Are jobs actually available near your home – or would you have to relocate? Are special skills needed such as typing or keying data? Is the job temporary or permanent? How much job security will you have? Is this a desk job, or will you travel?

Investigate the educational requirements needed to gain entry into a career field.

Some jobs require a college education – and graduate school. Some careers that require additional education will also require you to have financial assistance available. Be sure you know where you're going to get this money.

EDCON PUBLISHING

To achieve a career goal, you must know where you are going and set your sights high. But, you must be realistic. This requires matching your aptitudes, interests, and abilities, with your financial resources.

Once you have collected a great amount of data, you may become confused. That's when it's time to visit your counselor.

Ask your counselor to review your information and what you've accomplished so far. Are you on the right track? Do you need more information? What courses will prepare you for your career area? You might need a basic history, remedial math, or an advanced science course. Now is the time for you to ask these questions. Get your counselor's best educational advice.

Visit several local companies and determine what types of employment opportunities are available. This will help you decide which courses to schedule.

Course planning is really life planning. And to come up with a good plan, you need to accept the challenge responsibly by learning as much as possible about:

> **COURSE REQUIREMENTS**
> **GRADUATION NEEDS**
> **INTERESTS & ABILITIES**
> **CAREER INFORMATION.**

Use the problem-solving steps and begin as soon as possible to collect data. By doing this, you'll be able to take advantage of your school's curriculum and make meaningful and wise course selections.

The rest of your life depends on you organizing a plan of action. Why not begin today?

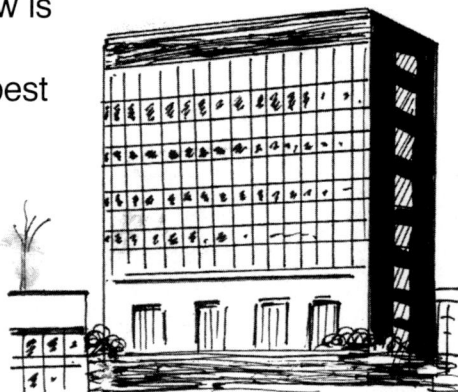

COURSE SELECTION
The Key to Your Future

LIST THE JOB OR OCCUPATION YOU ARE MOST INTERESTED IN PURSUING.

Use the framework below to collect information about this job. Use your library or Career Center. The Career Encyclopedia and the Dictionary of Occupational Titles (D.O.T.) are excellent sources.

1. General information about occupation: _____

_____

_____

_____

2. Education or training required:_____

_____

_____

3. Where employment may be found (geographics) and the need for persons skilled in this area:

_____

_____

_____

4. Wages/Salaries:_____

_____

_____

5. Where to obtain more information: _____

_____

_____

EDCON PUBLISHING

COURSE SELECTION

COURSE SELECTION
The Key to Your Future

What subjects are you going to study and for what career are you going to prepare?

_____

_____

_____

Which of the following curriculum areas interest you? Please check.

	YES	NO
1. Academic or College Prep?	____	____
2. Business or 2-year College?	____	____
3. Vocational or Trade?	____	____

Which of the following are your favorite subjects? Please check.

Subject	LIKE	DISLIKE	AVERAGE GRADE
English	____	____	_____
Social Studies	____	____	_____
Humanities/History	____	____	_____
Math	____	____	_____
Science	____	____	_____
Art/Music	____	____	_____
Physical Education	____	____	_____

Many occupations require either Math or English / History.

EXAMPLE: An engineer should be an **A** or **B** student, and have an interest in science.
A lawyer must like history and be an **A** or **B** student in English.

Which type of occupation do you prefer? One that works with:

1. data, figures?	___Yes	___No
2. people?	___Yes	___No
3. devices, mechanics?	___Yes	___No

Course planning is really life planning. Know your future goal and match your courses to fit your needs.

CHOOSING
A COLLEGE

EDCON PUBLISHING

CHOOSING A COLLEGE

After dinner, Patty headed to the local library when she saw Sarah walking toward her. "Hi, Sarah," said Patty. "Home from college?"

"Just visiting for the weekend," smiled Sarah warmly. "I have to go back on Sunday. How have you been?"

"Okay, I guess," answered Patty. "I'm thinking about going to college when I graduate. What made you decide to go to college?"

"Oh, a number of reasons, I guess. I wanted a better job than my mom had – to be somebody – to do something with my life. My boyfriend says he came to college to learn more about life – to liberate his mind, so to speak.

"On the other hand, his roommate just wanted to get away from home. While he's away, I don't think he's really committed to studying and learning, so he won't be there for long. College is fun, but believe me, it's hard work, too. But, now that you've made up your mind to attend, Patty, the hard part is still ahead of you – choosing the college that will best suit your needs."

CHOOSING A COLLEGE

"Yeah, I know," said Patty. "Miss Wicks, the school counselor, told me that the process for choosing a college is a lot like the one used to solve problems:

> 1. **Define the Problem**
> 2. **Collect Information**
> 3. **Propose Alternatives**
> 4. **Make Your Decision."**

"Yes," answered Sarah. "That's basically what you have to do. And everyone has to do it for themselves. It's really a personal thing.

"Perhaps your school counselor can help you with the next step – choosing the *right* college."

"That's a good idea," smiled Patty. "I think I will ask for her help. Well, I must be going before the library closes," said Patty. "See you soon – and good luck in college."

Patty, like a lot of our classmates, is faced with making one of the most important decisions of her life. Choosing the college that is "just right" will influence students the rest of their lives – financially, socially, and intellectually.

Each student will have to take on new and added responsibilities. They will face increased academic competition. They will have to learn how to manage their money and budget their resources.

They know that almost half of those who enter college – never finish.

So, to ensure success and save your family money, the reasons for choosing a college must be based on sound reasoning and effective decision making.

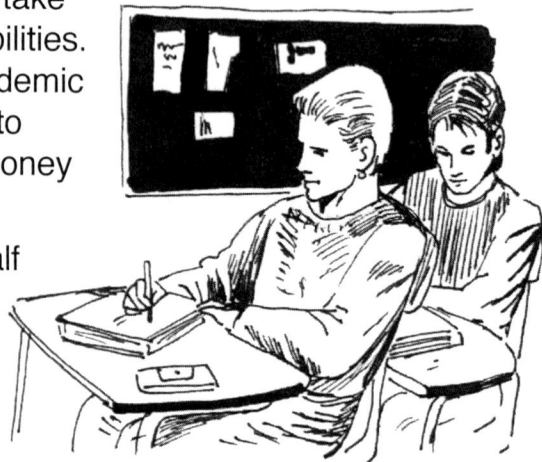

EDCON PUBLISHING

CHOOSING A COLLEGE

Patty enters the counselor's office. "Miss Wicks, I need some help. I've decided to go to college and now I'm not sure of my next step."

"Well, Patty," began Miss Wicks, "your next step is going to be a big one. So, let's give it some serious thought.

"You'll have to begin by collecting information in three areas:

1. **Your level of academic achievement**
2. **Your financial resources**
3. **Your major field of study.**

"And you must assume the responsibility for collecting this decision-making information. Nobody else can choose a college for you. It's really an individual thing. Others will help you but, in the end, it's your decision. So, can you stay for a few minutes? Maybe I can get you started."

"Sure," replied Patty. "I signed out of study hall and Mr. Martin knows that I'm here."

CHOOSING A COLLEGE

Miss Wicks gestured for Patty to take a seat.

"Selecting a major field of study is pretty important, isn't it Miss Wicks?" asked Patty.

"It certainly is," answered the counselor, as she reached for the school's course catalog. "Major fields of study are usually divided into basic groups. Let's take a look at them and three of their specialties.

AGRICULTURE
Agronomy
Animal Husbandry
Forestry

HOME ECONOMICS
Clothing/Textiles
Child Development
Food/Nutrition

BUSINESS
Accounting
Management/Administration
Marketing/Purchasing

HUMANITIES
Creative Writing/Literature
Philosophy/Religion
Speech

COMMUNICATION
Journalism
Radio/Television
Advertising

MATH and PHYSICAL SCIENCE
Math/Computer Science
Biology/Chemistry
Physics

FINE or APPLIED ARTS
Architecture
Art/Music
Dramatic Arts

SOCIAL SCIENCES
Law Enforcement
Social Work
Pre-Law
Psychology/Sociology

HEALTH PROFESSIONALS
Pre-Medicine
Nursing
Physical Therapy

EDCON PUBLISHING

Miss Wicks continued. "Often, students can't decide between two majors, so they will select a college that offers both. Then, after their freshman or sophomore year, they'll make a final decision."

"Well, I want to major in communications," said Patty, "but, I'm not sure if I'd like radio or television. I guess if I choose a college that offers both, I don't have a problem."

"That's true, Patty. I can see that you've been doing some thinking already – and that's great.

"We have a lot of college reference books and directories that you can use to learn more about individual colleges."

Miss Wicks reached for a book on the shelf behind her. "Now this college directory lists all the colleges by major fields of study. For example, if we turn to COMMUNICATIONS, RADIO AND TELEVISION, we see that all the 2-year and 4-year colleges that offer communications as a major are listed by state. This directory even lists the colleges that offer a bachelor's degree, master's degree, and doctor's degree in communications. You can quickly see that there are over 200 colleges that offer communications as a major field of study, so you're going to have to narrow down your choice a bit."

CHOOSING A COLLEGE

"That's really great, Miss Wicks. Let me write down the name of that college directory so I can find it later."

Miss Wicks went on. "The geographical locations of the colleges are another way to narrow down your choice. However, your next step is for you to talk to your parents about financing your college education. This could help you eliminate some of the schools that are out of your budget range, if you know what I mean."

"Yeah," smiled Patty. "I know what you mean. I better talk to Mom and Dad. Four years of college can get pretty expensive!"

Miss Wicks stood up. "Well, we're finished for today. You might as well get going to your next class. The bell is going to ring any minute. Remember to talk to your parents about finances and become familiar with the college directories in the Guidance-Resource Room.

"Next week during your study hall, we'll review your academic achievements."

EDCON PUBLISHING

Suddenly, the bell rang. Students filed out into the hall, making their way to their next classes, when Candice spotted Patty. "Hi, Patty, what's up?" she asked.

"Not much," answered Patty. "I was just talking to Miss Wicks about life after high school."

Candice chuckled. "Yeah, I had that same talk with her last week. She wanted me to think about what I was going to do two years from now. Heck, I have trouble deciding what I'm going to do for the weekend."

"I know what you mean," said Patty. "Two years seems so far off. But, Miss Wicks says the secret to success in choosing a college is advance planning. My problem is that there are so many colleges!"

"That's for sure!" said Candice. "And all of them are different."

"Well, I've got to get to class," said Patty. "Good luck with your planning, Candice. I'm sure Miss Wicks will help you. See you later."

After school, Patty talked with her mother. "I talked to Miss Wicks today about choosing a college."

"Miss Wicks is your school counselor, isn't she, Patty?" asked her mother.

"Yes, she is. She and I had a long talk about going to college in two years. She said that I should talk to you and Dad and find out if you could help pay for it. I guess it's pretty expensive."

"Well, Patty," said her mother, "your dad and I want to help pay for your college education, but we need to know how much it will cost."

"I could get a job and earn some money during the summer," said Patty. "Perhaps I could work at the college. And I can borrow some money to help finance my college costs."

"Well, we can make those decisions when we have a better idea of what the cost will be," said Patty's mom. "What college do you think you'll attend, Patty?"

"I'm not sure," Patty answered. "Miss Wicks will be going over my academic record with me next week. That will give me an idea of how I compare with other students attending college."

The following week, Patty sat down with Miss Wicks. "Well, Patty," said Miss Wicks, "today we're going to review your academic profile. I have all your records from first grade to the present in a cumulative folder. I've made a chart for you to look at with me. Your standardized test scores compare your achievements to other students' achievements. Well, let's see. . .in both reading and math you scored in the above-average range. Your scores also indicate that you are above average in verbal abilities, and your grades, which by the way are the best indication of college success, all seem to fall in the above-average range. You're in a college prep section, and you've taken some difficult courses."

"How will knowing that I'm a little above average help me to choose a college?" asked Patty.

"Well, every college has its own admission requirements and enrollment pattern. There are several college directories in the Guidance-Resource Room that you can use to match your academic profile with their Freshman Admittance Profile.

"Some colleges have an open enrollment policy and admit almost all who apply, while others are highly restrictive and admit only the top 5% of high school students."

EDCON PUBLISHING

"I see," said Patty. "My academic achievement level will help me narrow down the colleges where I can apply, get admitted, and eventually graduate."

"That's right," said Miss Wicks. "But, remember now, your academic achievements are only one variable in helping you narrow down your college choice.

"You'll want to know if the college is private or state related. State colleges will cost you less money, but sometimes it can be difficult to gain admission to them.

"It's important to know if the college is located in a rural or urban community, the number of students enrolled, the condition of the facilities, such as the library, the type of students who attend, and the types of resources available to students.

"Learning about the community can be accomplished by visiting the college. Before you make a final application, you and your family should visit the campus and community. This is the only way you can get a "feel" for the college.

"After you and your parents visit your top three choices, submit no more than three applications and, when you are accepted, notify all colleges of your final choice.

"And, lastly, some students select a college for its history and traditions."

"Boy, it sure is a lot of work choosing a college," sighed Patty. "Without your help Miss Wicks, I never would have been able to do it. If I follow your instructions, I'll be able to make a wise decision. Thanks so much."

CHOOSING A COLLEGE

Almost 50% of all those entering college will never finish. To ensure success and save your family money, the reasons for choosing a college must be based on sound reasoning and effective decision making.

STEP ONE - Making a Decision (Advanced Planning)

The first step in selecting a college is to collect information in three basic areas. What are they?

1. _____

2. _____

3. _____

MATCHING

Listed below are four (4) major fields of study. Place the major field of study letter, (S, B, C, H) next to its specialty. The first one has been done for you.

MAJOR FIELDS OF STUDY

(S) Social Studies (B) Business (C) Communications (H) Health Professionals

1.	Nursing	H
2.	Marketing/Purchasing	_____
3.	Law Enforcement	_____
4.	Radio/T.V.	_____
5.	Accounting	_____
6.	Pre-Law	_____
7.	Pre-Medicine	_____
8.	Journalism	_____
9.	Management/Administration	_____
10.	Advertising	_____
11.	Social Work	_____
12.	Physical Therapy	_____

Answers can be found on page 54.

EDCON PUBLISHING

CHOOSING A COLLEGE

STEP TWO - Financing

FILL-IN

Fill in the blanks in each sentence using the correct words from the box below.

tuition   assist   guidance   finances   attend   alternative

How much will it cost you to 1._____the college of your choice? Discuss 2._____ with your parents to find out how they can 3._____ you with 4._____. Discuss 5._____ financing (financial aide, student loans, and special grants) with your 6._____ counselor.

STEP THREE - Academic Achievement

Every college has its own admission requirements and enrollment patterns. Use the college directories to match your academic profile with their Freshman Admission Profile.

ACADEMIC ACHIEVEMENTS   **FRESHMAN ADMISSION PROFILE**

_____   _____

_____   _____

_____   _____

_____   _____

_____   _____

_____   _____

_____   _____

_____   _____

CHOOSING A COLLEGE

CHOOSING A COLLEGE

JUNIORS' TIMETABLE AND CHECKLIST

Place the correct date beside the item.

September ____1) Discuss the many aspects of life after high school with your parents, friends, teachers and counselors. Debate work vs additional education.

____2) Determine a first or second (Major or Minor) area of career interest. Develop a "Game Plan."

____3) Visit your school counselor and use the reference books for careers, colleges, trade, and business schools.

____4) Select 4 or 5 post-secondary schools that offer both your MAJOR and MINOR field of study.

October ____1) Take the Preliminary Scholarship Aptitude Test (PSAT). Several scholarships will use this test.

____2) Attend the college career fair at your local community college.

November ____1) Be sure you are scheduled for specific math, science, and/or foreign language courses that may be required for certain majors or specialized careers.

____2) Meet with union, business, college representatives when they visit your school.

December ____1) Talk with alumni during Spring Break about their jobs or post-secondary courses.

____2) Attend "Old Grads Day" at your school.

January ____1) Keep your vocational and academic grades high. Select colleges carefully. Take the highest level math course you can.

EDCON PUBLISHING

CHOOSING A COLLEGE

JUNIORS' TIMETABLE AND CHECKLIST
Place the correct date beside the item.

February   ____1) If you plan to enter a Nursing Program upon graduation, you must apply in your junior year to be considered for admission. This is also true for some Physical Therapy Programs.

March   ____1) Secure an application for the S.A.T. from your school counselor. Money must accompany the application.

April   ____1) Begin making plans for college visitation.
 ____2) Attend College Night(s) and Open Houses.
 ____3) Obtain approval from your vocational instructor in order to be eligible for Co-op experience.
 ____4) After you have verified eligibility for employment, you must begin working on your resumé.

May   ____1) Take the May S.A.T. _____(Date)
 ____2) Meet with your Co-op coordinator or career counselor to discuss local Co-op positions for which you would like to apply.

June   ____1) Plan vacation trips with parents so that you can visit colleges, trade, and/or business schools you are considering.
 ____2) Take the June S.A.T. _____(Date)

CHOOSING A COLLEGE

CHOOSING A COLLEGE

SENIORS' TIMETABLE AND CHECKLIST

Three choices after High School:

1. Work (Trade or Skill)

2. Education (Know MAJOR field of study)

3. Military (Join the Armed Forces)

October   ____1) Keep informed. Read Bulletin, Career Notes, and all bulletin boards. Check and double-check deadlines.

____2) Attend college, trade, and business presentations in which you are interested.

November   ____1) 1st mailing deadline for December S.A.T.

____2) Use the College Reference books in the Career Center to find the colleges that offer your **major** and **minor** fields of study. Write down the names and addresses of 4 colleges in which you are interested. As part of your initial November registration, you can send the results of the S.A.T. to four colleges for no additional fee. Make certain you select the ones you **really** are considering.

____3) Students interested in sources of financial aid should write for free publication. See your guidance counselor for address.

EDCON PUBLISHING

CHOOSING A COLLEGE

SENIORS' TIMETABLE AND CHECKLIST CONTINUED

December ____1) Secure and complete applications for colleges. Make certain you take all college and scholarship applications to your counselor **BEFORE** mailing.

____2) Begin completing Federal and State grant applications. **DO NOT MAIL.** Take these applications to your counselor for review. Financial aid applications cannot be mailed until January.

____3) Remember – all applications with a December or early January deadline should be given to your counselor at least 4 days before the beginning of Winter Break.

____4) Take the December S.A.T. _____(Date)

____5) **NON-COLLEGE BOUND STUDENTS** must complete the following: (1) typed resumé, (2) five completed job applications, (3) an application letter, (4) a letter of resignation, and (5) a video recorded job interview.

CHOOSING A COLLEGE

SENIORS' TIMETABLE AND CHECKLIST CONTINUED

January   ____1) In January, some colleges will offer tentative acceptances to outstanding students and/or students who are eligible for financial assistance.

____2) Always inform your counselor when you receive notices of acceptance or rejection from colleges or from scholarship agencies.

____3) As a senior, you will receive all types of "offers" for reduced rate tuitions, loans, listings in "Who's Who?" etc. Talk to your teachers and counselors and evaluate the worth of each offer. Don't let your ego spend your money! Think before you act.

____4) January is **FINANCIAL AID MONTH**. Attend all scheduled workshops and meetings on financial aid. After review by your counselor, make and keep a copy and mail the originals.

February   ____1) A copy of your 9-12 high school transcript (includes first semester grades) will be mailed to the post-secondary schools to which you have applied.

____2) Listen to announcements, watch bulletin boards, read Career Notes, talk to relatives, apply for scholarships and grants.

EDCON PUBLISHING

CHOOSING A COLLEGE

SENIORS' TIMETABLE AND CHECKLIST CONTINUED

March   ____3) Check all deadlines: College applications, scholarships, and/or financial aid. Remember, **YOU** have to pay back loans.

April   ____1) About this time, post-secondary schools will notify you whether or not you have been accepted. When you accept admission, notify your counselor and the other post-secondary institutions where you applied.

           ____2) Seek summer employment.

May   ____1) If you are not accepted by a post-secondary institution, and still desire to receive additional education, explore your options with your counselors.

           ____2) Check with the financial aid officer at the institution where you have been accepted. Sometimes "late" funding, jobs, or grants are obtained and you might "luck out." Also, if they know that you are trying to find money, they will be more likely to help you.

June   ____1) Final transcripts mailed.

           ____2) Please let your counselor know of your final job or college choice.

           ____3) Next year: (1) return the graduate follow-up survey, (2) contact your counselor for "Old Grads Day."

CAREER
DECISION-MAKING

EDCON PUBLISHING

CAREER DECISION-MAKING

"Dave, be sure to eat all your breakfast. And you had better wear a jacket. It's getting cold outside."

"Okay, Mom. But, I've got to hurry. I have an appointment with Mr. McGill, my school counselor, first thing this morning. Tell Dad I'll take out the trash when I get home tonight. So long."

* * * * *

CAREER DECISION-MAKING

"Good morning, Dave," said Mr. McGill. "Come on in. Have a seat and let's visit."

'Dave sat down in a chair. "Mr. McGill," began Dave, "I'm going to level with you. No matter how hard I try, I just can't seem to make a decision about next year's courses or my future career."

"Dave, I sense that you are feeling a little bit frustrated because you can't make a decision," responded Mr. McGill. "This is not uncommon. It happens to me and to many others.

"There is, however, a process that can be used as a framework for thinking about decisions. This process has 5 steps:

1. **DEFINE THE PROBLEM**
2. **GATHER INFORMATION**
3. **GENERATE ALTERNATIVES**
4. **SELECT GOALS**
5. **EVALUATE THE RESULTS**

"Let's start with Step 1, DEFINE THE PROBLEM. Now, this must be done in clear, specific terms."

Dave responded, "My problem is that I need to select courses for next year."

EDCON PUBLISHING

CAREER DECISION-MAKING

"That's right," replied the counselor, "and these courses should be related to your future career. You have your problem well defined.

"The next 2 steps are closely related – 2, GATHER INFORMATION, and 3, GENERATE ALTERNATIVES.

"Information is the "fuel" for effective decision-making. For a career decision, you must collect information about YOU – and about possible careers.

"Let's list some possible sources where you might get some of this information. Let's start with information about YOU."

"How about my teachers, my friends, my parents and possibly, you could help," said Dave.

"Well, yes," said Mr. McGill. "I can help, but you have mentioned some good sources.

"Now, when you begin to collect information about you, as an individual, there are three areas that you should concentrate on:

1. VALUES
2. INTERESTS
3. ABILITIES

CAREER DECISION-MAKING

"First, you should create a simple interview sheet. On one side, list your strengths. On the other side, your weaknesses. After you complete a sheet, make copies and give one to several friends, teachers, and relatives."

"Sure sounds like a lot of work," said Dave. "Is this information going to tell me what courses to take next year?"

"No, it's not that easy, Dave," said the counselor. "This will provide you with additional information about you that should help YOU make a decision.

"You must remember that, from now on, you're going to have to make more and more decisions. This process will help you, but it won't make decisions FOR you."

Mr. McGill stood up. "Let's get together in about a week and see how you're doing," he said, as he extended his hand to Dave for a handshake.

On the way home from school Dave dropped by Mr. Ross's house. Mr. Ross was one of his neighbors. *This is as good a time as any to get started*, Dave said to himself.

EDCON PUBLISHING

CAREER DECISION-MAKING

For the next week, Dave gathered whatever information he could from friends, neighbors, his parents and teachers. He was well prepared by the time he met with Mr. McGill again.

"Mr. McGill, I've collected the information we talked about last week."

"That's great, Dave," replied Mr. McGill. "Now, let's compare that information with your school cumulative folder. This should provide us with enough information to develop a profile or "picture" of you.

"Let's look at your ability first. Your grades are above-average, as are your tests of general ability. The achievement tests you took in 3rd and 6th grades seem to verify the fact that you are an above-average student. This would mean that you have enough ability to prepare for almost any occupation. By the way, what's your family's position on you attending college if you decide to further your education?"

CAREER DECISION-MAKING

"Both my mom and dad said they would help me financially if I wanted to attend college or a technical school. They will support me in obtaining any additional skills necessary to achieve my goal."

"Well, that's good," said Mr. McGill. "Now you don't have to limit your search for a career that does not require college. This does not mean that you HAVE TO go to college, but you can go if it's required for your area of interest. By the way, Dave, what are some of your areas of interest?"

"Well, I like swimming," smiled Dave, "and riding my bike, and basketball, and girls, too, I guess."

EDCON PUBLISHING

CAREER DECISION-MAKING

"Well, those interests certainly are normal," laughed Mr. McGill. "Your interests tell us that you like people and you like to be active. But, now it's time to review the decision-making process and see where we are. Again, the 5 steps are:

> 1. **DEFINE THE PROBLEM**
> 2. **GATHER INFORMATION**
> 3. **GENERATE ALTERNATIVES**
> 4. **SELECT GOALS**
> 5. **EVALUATE THE RESULTS."**

"Gee, Mr. McGill, we're still on step 2."

CAREER DECISION-MAKING

"Yes, that's right. But, remember that this is one of the most important steps and usually takes the most time.

"Now you must begin to gather information about possible careers." He handed Dave some booklets. "Here are several general booklets. After you have read them, stop by the Career Resource Room and talk to Miss Straub."

"Thanks a lot, Mr. McGill," said Dave. "Making a career decision sure isn't easy – even if you know how. But, I feel like I'm making progress."

* * * * *

The following afternoon Dave stopped by the Career Resource Room. "Good afternoon, Miss Straub."

"Good afternoon, Dave. I see you have your career cluster booklet with you."

EDCON PUBLISHING

"Yes," answered Dave. "Mr. McGill gave it to me to read. I didn't realize there were so many different occupations."

"There sure are, Dave," said Miss Straub. "In fact, the Dictionary of Occupational Titles lists over 35,000 different occupations.

"Although there are a number of ways to classify occupations, we prefer the career cluster approach – where groups of related occupations are clustered together.

"The career cluster approach permits a person preparing for an entry-level occupation to switch to another occupation within that particular cluster."

"Are you able to move up within a cluster?" asked Dave.

CAREER DECISION-MAKING

"Yes, Dave. Some people call it CLIMBING THE CAREER LADDER. You start at the bottom and, depending on your ability, interest, and performance, you move up toward the top."

"That's for me!" said Dave. "I want to move up fast. The people at the top make lots of money – and I like money!"

"Well," laughed Miss Straub, "earnings are certainly an important consideration but, here are eight factors you must consider when investigating a job:

44

CAREER DECISION-MAKING

1. EARNINGS
2. THE TYPE OF WORK PERFORMED
3. WORKING CONDITIONS
4. THE PHYSICAL DEMANDS OF THE JOB
5. SPECIAL TALENTS OR SKILLS
6. THE TYPE OF PREPARATION NEEDED
7. THE EMPLOYMENT PROSPECTS
8. JOB SECURITY."

"Boy, there's a lot to consider when you're learning about a particular occupation," said Dave.

"Yes, there certainly is," replied Miss Straub. "Plus, most jobs require you to be able to work with others, accept supervision, and be able to identify and cope with the expectations of the employer.

"Now, Dave, it's time for you to explore the career cluster. Remember, the 15 clusters are divided into job families and job functions. In getting started, I have students list their favorite school subjects."

CAREER DECISION-MAKING

"Favorite school subjects?" said Dave, with a puzzled look on his face. "How can they help me learn about jobs?"

"Well, Dave, your school subjects are clusters of learning," answered Miss Straub. "These learning clusters are related to certain job or career clusters. Let's look at a few examples:

CAREER CLUSTER: *Health*
USEFUL COURSES: *Natural Sciences; Math*

CAREER CLUSTER: *Business*
USEFUL COURSES: *Business Education; English; Social Studies*

CAREER CLUSTER: *Environment*
USEFUL COURSES: *Natural Sciences; Math; Agriculture."*

"I see," said Dave. "If I like math, I might investigate the HEALTH or ENVIRONMENT cluster."

EDCON PUBLISHING

"That's right," replied Miss Straub, "however, remember that this is just a general guide. Math and English are really basic subjects that are useful in almost any occupation.

"Dave, we have now reviewed things to consider when investigating occupations, and the use of school subjects as indicators of possible career clusters to choose from. But, where are you, Dave, in this decision-making process?"

"Gee, I guess I'm still on the second step–GATHERING INFORMATION," answered Dave.

"Well, that's the longest and, perhaps, the most important step in the process," the counselor remarked. "Once you complete this step, you must list some possible alternatives and select appropriate goals."

CAREER DECISION-MAKING

"But, Miss Straub, what if I complete the process and then I change my mind?"

"You've got to think of this as a continuous process," Miss Straub answered. "After you select certain goals, you will test them for appropriateness. This will provide additional information to use when proposing new alternatives and new goals. It's a continuous process, permitting you to change and grow as you proceed."

"It sounds like I have a lot of work to do," said Dave.

Miss Straub smiled. "Yes, you do, and you had better get started. Use the library, the Career Resource Room, interview friends and neighbors, and keep in touch with Mr. McGill."

Dave stood up to leave. "Well, thanks a lot for your help, Miss Straub. At least now I know how to proceed."

EDCON PUBLISHING

CAREER DECISION-MAKING

A. *To make a career decision, you must collect information. Below, list the three areas you should concentrate on when gathering information about yourself.*

1. _____

2. _____

3. _____

Now, start a profile of personal information.

MY VALUES ARE	MY INTERESTS ARE	MY ABILITIES ARE
_____	_____	_____
_____	_____	_____
_____	_____	_____
_____	_____	_____
_____	_____	_____
_____	_____	_____

CAREER DECISION-MAKING

B. There are 8 important factors you must consider when investigating a job. Can you name them?

1. _____

   _____

2. _____

   _____

3. _____

   _____

4. _____

   _____

5. _____

   _____

6. _____

   _____

7. _____

   _____

8. _____

   _____

EDCON PUBLISHING

Answer the following questions. You should know the answers when considering your career choice.

1. Do I know how to use the occupational clusters for exploration?

   ___Yes ___No

2. What are the strongest aspects of my personality?

   _____
   _____
   _____
   _____

3. Do I know my leisure time interests?

   _____
   _____
   _____
   _____

4. What are my strongest academic areas?

   _____
   _____
   _____
   _____

5. How much financial investment can I make?

   _____
   _____
   _____
   _____

CAREER DECISION-MAKING

Answer the following questions. You should know the answers when considering your career choice.

6. How long am I willing to attend school?

_____
_____
_____
_____

7. Do I know what to look for in selecting a job?

_____
_____
_____
_____

8. Can I get along with others?   ___Yes   ___No

9. Do I know my basic values?

_____
_____
_____
_____

List two of your favorite school subjects.

1. _____

2. _____

Research possible careers for each subject.

EDCON PUBLISHING

Notes

ANSWER KEY

CHOOSING A COLLEGE

STEP ONE - Making a Decision

1. Your level of academic achievement
2. Your financial resources
3. Your major field of study

MATCHING

2. B
3. S
4. C
5. B
6. S
7. H
8. C
9. B
10. C
11. S
12. H

STEP TWO - Financing

FILL-IN

1. attend
2. finances
3. assist
4. tuition
5. alternative
6. guidance

EDCON PUBLISHING

ANSWER KEY

CAREER DECISION MAKING

A.

1. values
2. interests
3. abilities

B.

1. earnings
2. work performed
3. working conditions
4. physical demands of the job
5. special abilities
6. preparation; further education
7. employment prospects
8. job security

Notes

EDCON PUBLISHING